Pauses
Along the Way

by Rob DiLillo

Pauses Along the Way

Copyright © 2023 by Robert DiLillo

All rights reserved. No part of this book may be used or reproduced in any manner whatsoever without written permission of the author except in the case of brief quotations embodied in critical articles or reviews. For more information or permission to reproduce, email info@RobDiLillo.com

Acknowledgments to the original publishers of several poems appear on page 75.

Contact information: info@RobDiLillo.com

Cover photo: Rob DiLillo
Author photo: Mary DiLillo

Visit RobDiLillo.com

Publishing History
First edition, 2023
Trade paperback ISBN 979-8-9882288-2-0

Published in the United States of America

For my father, Hugo Amadeo DiLillo,
who wanted to be a poet
and gave up so much for his family.

Part 1	**Wild Flowers**	
	Cool	2
	Desperation	3
	Hunter	5
	Peace/Spiders	6
	Everything White	10
	Pigeons	14
	tattooed	16
	Men	18
Part 2	**Coming to Ground**	
	Dove	24
	You were so beautiful	28
	Time to Go	30
	What I Gave	31
Part 3	**Yearning**	
	Melted	34
	Waiting	36
	The old brown fence	37
	I wish I had understood	38
	Flames	41
Part 4	**Journey of the Old Boat**	
	Intention	44
	stone buddha	45
	stone buddha II	46
	Borders	50
	Kiss	55
	If	56
	How Earth and Water Love	58
	How Water and Wood Love	59
	Once in Port Townsend	60
	Portland, 4am	63
	The Art of Serial Parting	64
	Waiting Again	66
	Fog	67
	First Rain	69
Part 5	**Another Step**	
	A New Story	72

Part 1 - Wild Flower

Cold eyes, piercing stare,
tall, strong limbs, feline moves
I return her smile

Cool

High style is cold
but I can't do cold or even cool.
I've tried to wear
black silver ice blue gray steel midnight
but something orange always sneaks out
protruding from a pocket
a red lining flashes
socks either yellow or bright green.

I should give up
be a clown
a house afire
a very wild flower.

Desperation

He -
All was still -
except your finger
a crazy cartographer on my chest
mapping my heart
with a slow blood-red nail
and my pulse
like solitary drops of water
exploding into a cup in the kitchen sink.

She -
We had just made love.
My legs were open, your sex sticky and wet,
heat surrounded us like heavy blankets
the moonscape ceiling reflecting
the orange light of a street lamp.
the crickets had stopped
a car passed slowly, killing the silence.

She clutched him to her chest and said,
"Sometimes, when I wake up in the middle
of the night like this,
I think only one thing can save me.
Afterward, I realize - nothing can save me."

Hunter

Black as despair
the cat waits patiently
against the white wall and gray concrete
muscles tense
yellow eyes electric mad
as sudden lightning.

When the black cat pounces on the unwary
there is never a sound
except the wailing victim
writhing in hooking claws and needle teeth.

I've seen the cat
play with his captive
waiting
talons extended
for a dash to safety
then striking
puncturing flesh
clutching dragging
its crippled prey relentlessly back.

This dark marauder likes to parade
with corpses in its mouth
and sometimes lays them
as offerings
at my door.

Peace/Spiders

A tiny red fellow hung
from a driftwood mobile in
the white kitchen sunlight
when the grapevines were shooting
and so was the corn.
I had just moved here
didn't know anyone, didn't care to
in the year of my peace with the spiders.

Slender web on a finger
fate in a hand
to crush 'neath a heel
or cast to the wind like a seed.
My son was born
five hundred miles away
and I didn't know him
barely knew her
and I was alone in the year
I had peace with spiders.

I opened the door
raised that spider to the gold morning sun
blew like a storm and said
"Go, eat flies!"
Then I smoked pot and worked on a book
about addiction and poison
and people alone
in my year of peace with spiders.

Spiders began to gather 'round my door
hang in corners
around my chair on the porch
where I read and wrote and smoked pot.

She called me one night
yelled for twenty minutes
then hung up.
And I could find nothing to say
in the difficult year
of my peace with spiders.

When the grasses turned golden
from the fresh green of spring
and spent webs
hung like dusty nooses from my ceiling,
I paid child support
lost two jobs, drank wine and was broke,
the year of my truce with spiders.

Flies buzzed the diner, Fred's Garage,
dodged swatters, newspapers and shoes,
yet I was protected by alliance and a
network of web.
At night, I haunted the neighborhood bar
for life or joy
or someone to share
this peace I had found with spiders.

I saved them from showers and sinks
and brushed them gently from corners
when their webs grew too thick.
Then I met a woman
with sky-blue eyes and wheat straw curls
who smiled at me with the hungry eyes
of a spider.

I fed one a June bug
her nest a white silken tunnel
in a crotch of a drain.
She loved me in a tent
On the Mendocino coast
when lightning danced
and rain poured down
one night in this summer of spiders.

A spider bit me as I slept
just once all the summer.
I'd killed one that morning
in the shower in my haste.
Now the spiders have left
because the cold rains have come
and she too is gone
and I am alone
with the hungry calm of a spider.

Everything White

He was unemployed in September. School had opened, and he had not found a teaching job. He slept on a foam pad on his balcony to escape the heat. Up with the sun, he walked two and a half miles into Glen Ellen for coffee. He picked up work painting apartments for his landlord, ten dollars an hour under the table. It was a wonderful job. White on white and the carpets to be replaced. No stress, no conflict, no decisions. Such a contrast to teaching.

Returning from town, he would strip to his grungiest shorts and oldest tennis shoes, fill a paint besmeared plastic water bottle, and head to work. An apartment door would be unlocked, and paint supplies stacked on canvas in the middle of the living room. He would open windows and put a mixtape in the boombox. It was easy work, white on white, carpet to be replaced. No molding or fancy trim.

He felt a channeling of energy in painting with the roller, a gentle stretching that unwound knotted muscles and blockages of the meridians. It felt meditative, the motions repetitive, a curving up-down stroke with the arms, bending to the paint tray. He would alternate, left hand then right, then both, reaching high on the upstroke, and sweeping low on the down. Sometimes, he would alternate and isolate muscles, do a stroke with the upper arm, a stroke where the shoulder bore the brunt of the work. One could even do a stroke featuring the lower back or that lightly worked the muscles of the legs.

His mind focused on movement and on a balanced spreading of both paint and work. He felt no problems no tension or no conflicts. He loved his music. Sometimes, he loved the quiet.

He drank a lot of water. He felt good. Happy. He ate brown rice and vegetables for lunch.

He painted everything white.

He painted over brown stains of blood and red stains of wine, over grime and ink and crayon. Over the dirty outline of furniture that used to be. He painted over white shadows where pictures used to hang. He painted over spent spiderwebs and smashed insects. He painted over food stains and mildew and scratches and gouges and cracks and dents.

He painted everything white.

He painted over grim memories and celebrations, over joy and embarrassment and disappointment. Over loneliness and lust. Over hopes. Over the sweat and breath of the people who lived in this place. He painted over hours and days. He painted over dust.

He painted everything white.

He painted over missing his son's birth and the cutting things she said, over the shattered sense he used to have of himself as a good person. He painted over grief and nightmares and hangovers and marijuana stupors. He painted over running away. Over the mean things he said. Over pettiness that hurt to remember. He painted over purple bruises of the spirit. He painted over guilt. Over despair. Over doubt.

He painted everything white.

He always wondered: who had lived here before, who would move in, and how would life within these walls be different?

He painted relentlessly, with all his being. And when he finished, he would clean his tools, go down to the apartment pool, dive into cool water and try to scrub off all that paint.

Pigeons

Live alone, do the housework.
Live alone, sit by yourself on Sunday afternoon,
staring out the window – remembering women,
in my apartment, in my bed, in my past.

A flock of pigeons
wheels in the sky,
          around buildings, trees
          and back again.
Country pigeons, clean, fat, and sleek,
not their raggedy concrete cousins from the city,
pigeons in finery with royal purple necks
tinted the spectral green of oil on water.

One spring, a couple tried to nest
on the air conditioner that juts from
beneath my window.
Whenever they landed,
I drove them away with a broom,
scattering the twigs they had piled
on the cold white metal
or I pounded the wall.
Their wings would squeak as they flew away.

This year
I heard their shuffling and scrabbling
and approached
determined to send them flying.

Then I stopped.
If there was room for spiders
and black cats
why not pigeons?
To see a home built,
hear mates cooing and
young ones squeaking in the nest.
To watch bustling parents on their errands
might be better than being alone.

So, I waited, wondering if pigeons ate spiders.

Perhaps my singing in the shower
was loud and off-key.
Perhaps, being country pigeons,
they were not fond of Miles Davis.
Perhaps the cold, bare metal
offered no proper foundation for a home.
Or perhaps they were the same pigeons from last year,
for they sat in the warm sun,
flew off,
and never returned.

tattooed

On the phone she told me
she planned to break up with him
then He pounded the door

He wanted to show her - her face
tattooed on his right arm, eternally His
rippling and reacting to His every move

i don't know what to say

I do. I love you baby

i wish you hadn't done that

what do you mean?
tensing His arms
her face there scowling, contorting
into an expression she had never worn

i mean it's very sweet

I want to be sweet to you baby
come to me
I've been thinking about you all day
every time the needle went in

she wanted to say no
but when she looked into her own eyes
a grimace
a shaking of the head
warned her
that those muscles
had lifted thousands of pounds of iron
iron like in chains and manacles
and prison bars
for just the moment
when she was to say no
to slug Him in His pride
knock some ego out of Him

when He thrust himself
inside her
she felt as though she had been
thrust inside some dark narrow place
from which there was no escape
and there wasn't
she knew there wasn't.

Men

Men are tainted by the worst in us.

We can go wrong in so many ways.
We can be bumbling incompetents
who fail over and over again.
Crippled by doubt, stinking with fear.

We can be faithless, dishonest,
      stubborn beyond reason, irrational,
      mad with drink, drugs, dogma,
      chaos, confusion,
      restless, irritated,
      seething with aggression.

We can be consumed by greed,
      reckless with it, owned by it,
      corrupted so that we trample all else we value.

We are dying to be loved.
We twist ourselves,
      aching for acceptance and confirmation.
We can be perverse,
      lustful with gory horns of the beast.
We can be lonely, moonless night lonely, poised on
the lip of violence to ourselves and others.
We hold caldrons of bubbling anger, laced with
shame, steaming in guilt while we plot and lie.
We drink cups of poison regret.

We can be low down, mean, and hopeless.
We abuse.
We rape.
We torture.
We make the sin of war.
We oppress with great skill and cruelty.
We are, all of us, stained by this.

But this is not all we are.

We love, oh how we love, ferociously, fearlessly.
We love like wood loves fire
    burning ourselves completely
    so that nothing remains.
We try to the last ounce of our strength.
We stand loyal, dedicated
    to that which seems worthy.
We serve,
    give our lives for our beliefs,
    for our families, for lovers.
We do our duty.
We provide.
We protect.
We nurture, support, and listen.
We take care.
We husband.
We honor.
We humble ourselves.
We pray.
We strive in a thousand ways
    to reach harmony with divinity.

We are innocent.

We laugh in the midst of blood-soaked war-torn
    hopelessness.
We laugh with delight.
We laugh at death.
We laugh at ourselves.
We laugh at those who would oppress us.
We men are filled with this.

We work.
We sweat and bleed and break our backs,
break our hearts, rot our bellies.
We strain to the utmost of our beings and
accept the impossible as our labors.
We conquer pain
We overcome, we overcome, we overcome,
    day after day.
    year after year.
We persevere
even when we know for certain we can't go on,
when all the world commands us stop.
We are men, made for this.

We think and wonder and dream and imagine.
We solve problems one after another without end.
We create and innovate
with the boldness and genius of a god,
with the single-minded purpose of seeds.

We create beauty,
    harmony,
    wonders of technique and invention
    our forefathers would consider miracles.
We create families, gardens,
companies, societies, and principles.
We teach.
We heal.
We accept the grim and awesome responsibility of
    destruction.
We men are born to create.

We are both aware and oblivious.
We do not understand ourselves or our power.
We are bold and comic.
We spread our courage like the light of suns.
We feel empathy.
We rebel and obey,
    lead and follow,
    plan and reflect.
We traverse the world and our souls,
trying to find the beloved.
We are holy.
We are strong, our hearts filled with joy,
our spirits with wonder.

We are men.

Part 2 – Coming to Ground

> Fly over mountains?
> I can't. You see I'm
> waiting for the bus.

Dove

My briefcase squeaks like the wings of a dove
as I walk to school
amazed that the alchemy of years
has transformed me from student to teacher.
I go to preach my peace
to the young men and women
who simply want to get through history
through this unit on
the moldering remains of the '60s
with as little fuss as possible
sparks of passion rare
as tie-dyed shirts
idealism sleepy and stoned
and no hallucination
that the world can be transformed
or that life has any meaning
beyond pleasure and security.
Join up, tune in, zone out.

My briefcase creaks like old bones
skeletons swaying in the closet.
They buy everything:
   bourgeois aspirations
   consumer culture
   that a good job is the purpose of education.
They wear advertisements on their shirts.

And I know I am old fashioned
because I cling to antique notions:
　there is salvation in art and free thinking
　one can create exactly the kind of life
　　　one can imagine
　if enough of us look into our hearts
　　　and conscience the world will be transformed
　this is the dawn of a new age where tolerance and
　　　kindness will win over fear and power
　we stand on the verge of actualizing our ideals
　this will someday be the land of people
　　　brave enough to live in harmony
　　　to chase their happiness down whatever wild
　　　wonderful dangerous roads it may lead.

My key in the lock of the classroom
sometimes feels like the jailhouse door
kids forced into seats
a place of both honor and shame
elevated by Henry David and Dr. King.
There will be 30 of them
　bored expecting little
　hoping for entertainment
　a bit of racy trivia
　or maybe an idea to cling to in the rough seas
　　　of decades later.

I want to say something
   about beautiful naïve idealism
   the searing fire of change
   about battling the old power
   and losing
   and giving in when you couldn't take anymore
   about big defeats and small victories
   about the slow plodding of history.

Headphones thump
like electronic heartbeats
as they troop from class
a psychedelic blend of ethnicities
who wonder why everyone couldn't just get along.
I wonder what they think
about the old fart mystified by ideals?

Except for the girl wearing a granny dress
and combat boots
   with an Earth First patch on her backpack
   a nose ring
   and barbed wire tattooed around her wrist
who says as she steps into the sunshine
"It would have been so cool to live back then."

You were so beautiful
when you were pregnant.
I couldn't keep my hands off you
took pictures of the curve of your belly
the fullness of your breast
     your radiance.

I liked to gather you up
like a child gathers delight
     and urge you toward soft places
     the freshly painted white
     and California light of that cottage
         where we nested.

When you were six months along
you took us to the Sequoias
of Calaveras
a place your mother loved.
On our last hike
you left me behind
and ran away from me
down through the trees
in the gold-slanted light
in your orange flip-flops
with Rosalyn Sierra in your belly.

We had us a Virgo
who loves running and mountains
and forest and animals.

You kept those flip-flops a long time.
Whenever I saw them
      in the closet
      on the back steps
      in the rocks by the river
I would bow my head
and smile
and remember how
beautiful you were when you were pregnant
and how happy.

Time to Go (for Rosalyn)

The wind carries voices across the water,
indistinct murmurings,
shadows of words,
a pulsating bullfrog,
a mockingbird's trill.
The sun's last glance sparkles on ripples,
suspended between day and night.

She plays on the edge of deep water,
sings odes to all she sees,
presses flowers between two flat stones,
because even at six years old
she senses herself passing
through a sweet honest time
which fear and ambition will soon wash away.

The wind carries voices across the water,
words the weight of ghosts.
I watch her crouched on the earth
wild hair blowing,
in love with azure sky,
animals, flowers, and the rocks that press them.
To her, each thing contains its own joy,
touched by the hand of
some innocent, beautiful goddess.

Voices shout across the water,
significant as the sunset.
I long to hear them,
to have wise, magical words for her
before darkness engulfs us
and it's time to go.

What I Gave

Days roll past like breaking waves.
My hands hold only what I make,
and the years yield only what I gave.

I search the sands for what I crave,
filled with a lonely, longing ache.
Days roll past like breaking waves.

Hours once gone cannot be saved.
Time-worn memories I would take,
but the years yield only what I gave.

Black ocean deep will storm and rave.
The tide of minutes we cannot break,
so my days roll past like breaking waves.

Salt sea winds I've dared to brave.
Dreams aground and hopes forsake.
The years yield only what I gave.

Promises broken and promises grave.
I may stride strong or my legs may shake,
but the days roll past like breaking waves,
and the years yield only what I gave.

Part 3 – Yearning

Under the quiet
roars a hushed cacophony
that sounds like silence

Melted

We lost power.
It's bone-shaking cold.
Everyone is asleep,
but I'm at the table
fascinated by candles.

Have you ever held two candles together?
The flames join and rise higher and brighter
than each alone.

Have you ever thought about taking that
naked flame, touching it
    to curtains and furniture
    and riding that certain heat
    that bright light
    that fury and fantasy
    and ugly black smoke
    all the way to the moon?

Have you ever thought that
Fire is more honest than people?
It simply burns
while we can be so many things.
Have you ever stayed up
Shivering, bone shaking,
watching the wax puddle,
cold fingers cupped around
a stub of a candle
because it was the only light
and you couldn't bear to blow it out?

Waiting

Sonoma afternoon -
old farmhouse, ancient windmill
black crow, blue sky
golden light, white half-moon
silver wood of a phone pole riven by time
drilled by woodpeckers
black wires splayed
sycamore shade
variegated bark
falling leaves
strutting quail
busy wife
dancing leaves, delicious breeze
distant traffic tears the quiet.

I moved here for
this peace, this beauty
but how the frantic windmill spins
and cries
out of balance.

The old brown fence
came down
collapsing completely
like a long-held illusion.
On the other side
stood a world I'd forgotten,
a slate gray pond
wild sweet blackberries
graceful willows and dancing grass.

I thought about forcing the fence to stand
propped with posts and beams
cobbled together with wire and nails
    I weighed expense and labor
        concrete and holes in the clay.

But it was rotten wood
crumbling
some of it stained green
with copper poison
not even fit to burn.

I stood for a long while
worrying about my lost fence
and watching the pond turn blue
as the clearing sky.
I remembered -
I never really liked fences,
so I stepped across old boards
and down to the edge of the pond
and took off my clothes
    and slipped into the cool dark water.

I wish I had understood so many things:
that good people will not necessarily help each other thrive
how we could work so hard to build a life and create a home and raise a strong, kind, determined, soul-beautiful child without really connecting.
how hard work crowds out intimacy
how a fine home and yard are not as important as building a relationship and how much maintenance is required to sustain one
how compartmentalizing things that give us pain pulls people apart
how essential it is to consciously grow together
how much I value dynamic conversation
how exactly the strength of a relationship mirrors the degree of communication.

I wish I had known:
how little I understood my own feelings and to touch each emotion as it rises
how emotional pulling away isolates us
how peace is nice but engagement no matter how strained or difficult, leads to growth
that asserting myself would have helped us flourish
how important it is to share common interests because shared joy holds a couple together
how integrity demands we be our own best selves
that I am responsible for my own happiness and you were not
that happiness is a choice or, more accurately, a series of choices.

that to share a successful life without, you must share
   the life within and to do that, you must know your
   heart and the forces that shaped it.

It would have improved my marriage
had I been better at
   speaking my truth
   pausing before reacting
   reading the geography of spaces between partners
   knowing you were doing the best you could
   and that I was, too.
understanding how damaged you were
   how damaged I was
   and how all that damage came between us.

I wish I'd been aware of:
all the ways of being contained in the words
   'husband' and 'wife' and that each is a complex,
   independent person outside of these roles.
how much conventional thinking I rebel against
the courage I lacked
how the safe path leads to stagnation
how free I was all that time without even realizing it
how you can live any way you want
how we are our own works of art,
   created every moment of every day
   with each word, choice, deed, and thought.

Flames

When candles lean together
two flames join
lifting the body of light
dispelling mist from the mind's eye.

When candles tilt apart
brightness widens like a river
reaches into silences and dark corners
to reveal the body of night.

Part 4 – Journey of the Old Boat

> He saw not body
> not face, life, habits, or eyes
> he just saw spirit

Intention

I shall go to sea in an old boat.

Once a working boat
for fishermen and traders
with strong timbers
crafted by keen eye and
skilled hands

this old boat survived
storms
heavy burdens
long journeys

and maybe one more
to the Land of Light
with its Gold Mountain
where the sun is born
and the Elixir of Life flows
from the roots of a magic tree.

stone buddha

I wrapped my arms around
the white and black stone Buddha.
When I lifted, the weight of him
bent my back and took my breath.

Damn, that's one heavy Buddha,
as much as I can carry.
I bore him through
the rooms of my life,
garage, kitchen, dining room, bedroom
to the garden where I meditate.

I sat on my cushion before him,
(The Buddha needed no cushion)
my back nearly as straight as his
but my face
was not as gentle or as peaceful,
strained by
the weight of things that happened,
things I might do,
words I might say,
words I might regret,
and eyes blue, deep, and complicated
as Puget Sound.

stone buddha II

the path beyond the stone buddha
bends out of sight

Inhale
i wish it led to you
like when i open my computer
hoping you've left words
    Thinking

Exhale
stones and sand
green leaves and fragrant lavender
the rip and roar of distant traffic
white glare off leaves of the lemon tree

Inhale
a squirrel chattering
bird song
bees buzzing
red stones embedded in sand

Exhale
the path bends out of sight
your smile and pale skin would fill the
garden
    Thinking

Inhale
i fear i wrote so poorly
you won't know how i felt.
i don't trust my words
or you won't
but you always
    Thinking

Exhale
understand
the cool morning breeze
caresses my skin
you are so gentle with me
so incredibly gentle
    Thinking

Inhale
two birds chase each other
around the pear tree
that bends under dark red fruit

Exhale
the path of red stones
curves out of sight
the distant roar of a plane
the blur sound of a hummingbird's wings
sun glinting off mica in the sand

Inhale
wish you would come down the path
smiling
    Thinking
bird song and traffic

Exhale
green leaves, bright sun
cool shadows
the breeze caresses my skin
the hum of bees
the buddha doesn't move

Borders (with Lisa McIvor)

As they stepped through a door
into a minatory red twilight
born of fire and a coming storm,
he wanted to tell her
that boundaries are liminal spaces.

Sometimes,
borders are indistinct and exist only on a map,
wilderness stretching in all directions.
In other places, they are guarded by walls,
men with weapons,
the seductive scent of
pink purple blossoms
growing over barbed wire,
smelling like the plums they may soon be.
Borders can be dangerous places
of longing and regret.

When you cross a border
something opens to let you in.
Something opens inside you.
But you don't know the roads and the places
on the map are merely names
of uncertain meaning.

Grief and love are not separate countries,
yet when you cross over
the land releases a different spice,
the sky is a peculiar blue,
and homes are constructed in a foreign language.

Their walls carry an unfamiliar texture,
with different words on them in oddly shaped letters.
You walk through streets wary of eyes that linger,
and even the color of dust is new.
You search for ways to survive.

She wanted to say,
Sometimes boundaries are all we know of love.
We inhabit the smallest country of ourselves,
bordered nations of bone and breath,
name ourselves as edge and line.

Sometimes we spill newborn,
borderless and alone, fleeing
guns and explosions in the razored night,
having lost the requisite papers, our passport,
that last bit of cash tucked inside our shoe.
We become continents of shadow,
refugees of meager light far from home.

The riverbank of the heart reaches
always toward the ocean,
it aches for an almost forgotten tide
and its smooth stones weep for salt.

Will we become a brine of soft bodies
in the storm's silvered aftermath, castaways,
beached to the threshold of our fingertips,
naked as the limits of our skin?

Or will we discover meeting places
along the borderlands,
paths hidden under the trees, winding
up the spine of hills?

In half-light, she hoped that
walls might become bridges,
and fists might open, beckoning them to shelter.

They saw, along the wall, a thousand cracks
where children had carved small windows,
and filled them with crumpled flowers
in colors of sunlight and blood,
love letters,
words like 'remember' and 'holdfast',
folded between the stones.

He said, "Here I will always be kissing you."

They paused at the place of fissure,
root of the path winding
between shards of broken stone,
She shivered in the chill of the wall's shadow
and whispered, "Here, I will be always waiting."

Kiss

One rainy Seattle day
we rose from a table
of the Bauhaus Cafe
drunk
on each other's eyes
    and the Earth folded
    and a locus of gravity
    drew us together

I bent my head
you rose on your toes

And our lips
naked except for
lavender jasmine tea
and honey
and your pink lipstick
met

We pretended
that the cafe didn't crumble
walls collapsing
and the carpet of gold
and crimson leaves on the sidewalk
didn't float back to their branches and turn green
and the bare black earth of the
planter boxes didn't fill with flowers
and the Seattle mist didn't turn to golden glitter
and drain the clouds
to blue sky
and that I could ever board
a plane and leave you.

If

If I were a dream
at first light on a brilliant spring morning,
I would wake you slowly
with a gentle hand on your head
and incantations of wonderful.
I'd turn on your bedside lamp and show you
a small brass key
to a box painted impossible colors
you had long forgotten
hidden by books
in the recesses of your closet.
Inside would be a locket
whose ovaled window
held the face of the woman
you hoped to become.

If I were love
on a sleepless summer night,
I would pour cool breeze
through your window
to brush against the moonlight of your cheek.
In a voice like cicadas and frogs,
I would tell you a story
about lovers in the tall grass,
a plum's dark sweetness,
unexpected rain, running, and laughter.

If I were peace
on a dark autumn afternoon,
crimson and yellow leaves against a gray sky,
I would wander through your kitchen door,
wearing a joyous grin
and hug you into the warmth
of my open coat.
I would linger in the pumpkin ginger soup
simmering on the stove,
in the darkness of coffee beans
resting fragrant on your shelf.
Then I'd settle myself in the red geraniums
clustered in a chipped yellow bowl
that had been your mother's
to watch over you as the light faded.

If I were faith
on a cold winter night,
I would rise like steam from your bath
and curl around you.
I would wash fear away with
with strong hands and a rough cloth
then wrap you in soft white towels
and the scent of lavender
that you and your true love will plant
in a garden you have to yet see.

How Earth and Water Love

Earth absorbs her
contains her
gives her flow and borders
He cradles her
inviting her into
his deepest places

Water comes to him and leaves
floods him with her presence
shrivels him in her absence

Sometimes trickles over him
and sometimes rages
smooths his rough edges
carries bits of him away

She softens him
cools him
and gives him fecundity

This delights them both
into flowers and great trees
into fawns gamboling in a meadow by a brook
into the lion crouched
on a limb
Intent

Don't they dance beautifully?

How Water and Wood Love

She fills him
nourishes him
makes him who he is

He pulls her
from deep places
raises her to light

Together they become
leaf and flower, fruit and seed
all things crafted from wood

To love her
is to love the creator
How could he not?

Once in Port Townsend

A door creaked open
with the brisk song of a bell
to a shop whose ancient walls
were filled with thread in
strutting peacock blue,
emerald, the shade of her eyes,
bruised purple,
and skeins of yarn
waiting to be woven, tangled, and tied.

A narrow staircase
rose to a loft of shadows,
and the late afternoon sun filtered
golden through high windows
to a spill of dust motes.

Behind an antique cash register,
the young clerk sat reading
a paperback romance.
We must have had sparkles
in our eyes, worn sweet, wild grins.
"What are you two up to?"
she asked, arching an eyebrow.

He whispered,
"Can you keep a secret?"

He waited for her certain nod
before adding, "With this ribbon
the color of blood,
we will entwine
our wrists in a promise
and bind ourselves as soulmates,
reunited after who knows how many
lifetimes.
If you keep the secret,
you shall find yours."

Then he winked and added,
"Keep the change."

Portland, 4 am

Of course, it was cold, dark, and rainy
in Portland at 4 am.
Ken's bakery wasn't open
and they had drunk no coffee.
They could smell it being brewed inside
and chocolate baking and the caramelizing
of sugar and butter and flour.

There was only one thing to do.
So, he guided her to a dry doorway
pressed her against the bricks
and kissed her.
And he liked it so much he kissed her again.
And he found he couldn't stop.
And because he was so driven to kiss her
he thought he ought to try stopping,
and when he finally succeeded
and looked around at the rain,
red and green lights
decorating the wet street of 21st Avenue
like Christmas
and the old brick apartment buildings,
all of them seemed to be asking him one
kindly meant question: "Why did you stop?"
He had no good answer, so he kissed her again,
knowing that soon
they would board planes heading
in different directions.

The Art of Serial Parting

We are always leaving each other,
getting into cars, shuffling aboard planes,
hanging up the phone.
It helps to pretend it doesn't break my heart
a little every time,
to pretend it doesn't haunt me from the moment
you arrive.
But people adapt to anything, don't they?
Normalize. It's a coping mechanism.

Remember when I read
"Time in a Bottle" to you
and couldn't finish through the tears?
Maybe all relationships contain
turning away to dwell in the self.
Maybe loving like this we are spared the little cuts,
dozens of daily 'It's about me now all on my own.'
We have both lived through that slow separation.

Therapists want our love
to follow a pattern, statistics, studies.
They want to have words for it.
Labels.
I once thought
it would be comforting to be diagnosed,
to have a condition with tendencies,
a known course to follow.

We tried to write that poem, Ghosts,
but you are the ghost
the spirit hovering
    over my shoulder
    in my head
    behind my ribs
the ghost that captures me
unawares in the most innocent moments.
And I am your ghost.

We choose this life,
    you and I,
    to love this uncertain, vulnerable way.
We open to each other like flowers,
blooming only a short time every year.
Or maybe we are like climbers,
bold and confident in our ability to be an us,
tiptoeing the edge,
on terrain invisible from the highways and main paths
then letting ourselves fall
in serial parting.

It makes you strong, standing alone,
he thinks as he watches her walk away,
strong and lonely.

Waiting Again

I haven't lost you yet
if not counting the hours
makes time flow backward
minutes whipping past in reverse
    days
        months
            years.

it is not yet winter.
trees still cling to
leaves of bright yellow and red.
autumn pinpricks of Seattle drizzle
dot the film of water
on the windshield's blurred glass
and fade to a clear
almost nothing.

there is no safety anywhere in the world
except, maybe, in your eyes,
certainly not in these specks of water,
    these innumerable thousands.

each drop makes its mark
fades into a film.
each moment passes
and the answer lies
not in my heart's desire
but in rain
sliding down the glass.

Fog

at 30 thousand feet
fog shines white
in the low places
fertile valleys appear locked
in glacial ice

once upon a time
you would fly from the northern drizzle
to me
in the sunny wine country
but now I come to you from the
other direction

you feel our home in the sun
is haunted by ghosts
while I feel a heavy fog pressing
against the windows
of the temporary shelter you offer

at 30 thousand feet
peaks rising from the fog
and capped with snow
are nowhere near as cold
as knowing
after all this time
that your home is back there
mine is far away

and this was our choice.

First Rain

Northern California
in autumn
after parching summer
first rain raises
the scent of dust
thirsting to be mud,
the scent of ash.

Dead golden grass
grateful at last to bow
to the weight of water
releases the burden of standing tall.

Blades and stalks long to sink
into Earth's embrace
into her soft flesh
sensing that only in surrender
will they rise.

Part 5 – Another Step

Travel down the road
a little bit further and
you will see the way

A New Story

It's disorienting,
shifting
from one story to another.
Turn the page and the world changes,
perspective transforms.
Mysterious strangers displace well-known characters.
Longing to decipher them, you turn away from
people who once captured your heart.

Going from one story to another
is like materializing in a different painting,
cast in a new style with disparate shades and colors,
composed by a distinct hand.
You explore new ground,
hike different trails and linger in unfamiliar haunts
which come to feel like home.
You learn an alternate vocabulary
and live surrounded by odd furniture
and unusual books
in rooms you never imagined and slowly
the memory of antique places fades.

I found the book of you
in a random cafe
and opened the cover
to your diamond eyes and kind smile,
while you ordered the breakfast
I intended for myself.
You were straightforward, thoughtful, articulate,
easy to read -
full of sad, hard tales where the protagonist
fought her way through one trouble after another,
with a wry smile and easy laugh,
always emerging stronger, wiser,
ready for another challenge.

When I reached for that very private shelf
to give you the book of me,
you didn't read a few pages
and set it on the nightstand or coffee table
but kept reading,
and eventually added a chapter of your own.

About the Author

Rob DiLillo is a west coast writer and teacher with roots in Los Angeles, Berkeley, Portland, and Sonoma County. His writing center of gravity is the Centrum Writing Community. He has published a mystery novel, *Night People*, set in Portland in 1980 with a sequel to come, and a literary novel, *Be My Heroin*, also set in Portland. He has published poetry, fiction, and essays in various journals.

Visit RobDiLillo.com

Acknowledgements

Backchannels Journal published an early version of "How Earth and Water Love."

Book of Matches Literary Journal published "Peace/Spiders."

The Royal Prune published "Borders."

Borders was co-written with Lisa McIvor who has published two poetry collections, *Winter Mother* and *Breathe.*

This work owes a huge debt of gratitude to Sharon Kirk for the cover design, formatting, her exacting editor's eye, her determined encouragement, and so much more.

Lisa McIvor taught me so much about the nuances of poetry. I would not have been equal to this work if she hadn't helped me grow both as a writer and a human being.

Made in the USA
Middletown, DE
07 February 2024